This journal was completed by

_____

and

_____

Date: _____

Conversations with My Dad

Conversations
with
My Dad

A Keepsake Journal
of Stories and Memories

LARK
New York

New York

An Imprint of Sterling Publishing Co., Inc.
1166 Avenue of the Americas
New York, NY 10036

ISBN 978-1-4547-1065-3

Distributed in Canada by Sterling Publishing Co., Inc.
c/o Canadian Manda Group, 664 Annette Street
Toronto, Ontario M6S 2C8, Canada
Distributed in the United Kingdom by GMC Distribution Services
Castle Place, 166 High Street, Lewes, East Sussex BN7 1XU, England
Distributed in Australia by NewSouth Books
45 Beach Street, Coogee, NSW 2034, Australia

For information about custom editions, special sales, and premium and corporate purchases,
please contact Sterling Special Sales at 800-805-5489 or specialsales@sterlingpublishing.com.

Manufactured in Canada

2 4 6 8 10 9 7 5 3 1

Interior design by Shannon Nicole Plunkett
Cover design by David Ter-Avanesyan and Shannon Nicole Plunkett

Spot Art
iStock: © AllAGRI; © Elinalee; © Inkant; © katyakatya; © Ekaterina Romanova; © Galina_Cherryka

Contents

Introduction

For as long as you've known him, your dad (or any father figure in your life) probably has told you stories about himself. Perhaps you've gotten a glimpse of his childhood when he shares a favorite memory from his elementary school days. Or there's been a time when you ask a question that prompts him to recall one of his wildest adventures. But maybe you and your dad talk less frequently than you'd like. Or there are large parts of his life that have remained a mystery and that you want to know more about. Whether you have a treasure trove of information about your dad or only one or two insights, you might find yourself wondering what his dreams for the future were as he was growing up, how he felt when he moved away from home for the first time, or what he wants to pass down to the next generation.

Conversations with My Dad is here to help you answer those questions and discover even more. This book is designed to be a keepsake, but it's more than a record of dates or a repository of photos. On each page, you'll find thoughtful prompts that are designed to spark a rich and ongoing dialogue with one of the most important people in your life.

Many of the questions in this book go beyond the facts and conjure vivid memories and exciting stories from your dad's life—some of which you might have never heard before. They will encourage him not only to describe what happened but also tell you how he experienced that event, what he thought about it, or what he thinks about it now. It's likely these questions will encourage you to ask questions of your own or share your personal experiences. As you go through these pages, you'll laugh at his funniest tales, reminisce about the times you've spent together, and celebrate the unique story that is his life. With *Conversations with My Dad*, you'll learn more than you'd ever expected.

How to Use This Book

Because each father-child relation-ship is unique, each conversation will be as well. How you and your dad use this book to record the conversa-tions it prompts is personal, but to help get you started, here is some information to make the experience of completing this book meaningful.

The Art of Conversation

The first and most important premise when using this book is simply this: trust your instincts and follow your heart. You and your dad might prefer to take a look at the inviting blank spaces in this book and fill them in as quickly and efficiently as possi-ble. Or the two of you might want to work your way through the questions more slowly and over the course of several sessions. You might want to work through the book sequentially or go out of order, depending on what topic interests both of you on a par-ticular day.

No matter what approach you take, the important thing to remember is to create a comfortable space and allow enough time to nurture a genuine conversation whenever you work on the book. Brew some coffee or tea, sit in comfortable chairs, and put your daily obligations on hold so you can savor the conversation.

It's also helpful to remember this essen-tial piece of advice: Don't assume! Listen with fresh ears to even the most famil-iar stories of your dad's life. You may be surprised at what another retelling might reveal. Don't be afraid to ask what seems to be an obvious question. The answer often turns out to be one that you hadn't anticipated at all.

How Much to Write

Some of the questions in the book feature blanks for recording straightforward details about the milestones and people in your dad's life, from his first word to the names of his grandparents. Many of these answers might be easy to capture entirely right there on the page.

Most often, though, you'll find open-ended questions, the kind that will bring vivid and detailed memories to mind. The richer the vein a question hits, the less likely it is you'll have enough space on the page to record your dad's answer word for word. Record what you feel is the essence of the conversation—the evocative details, the special nuggets, the heart of what an experience meant to him. If there's something you want to write more about, turn to the "More Stories" section at the end of the book (see page 106). These open pages in the back of the book allow you to say more about a certain subject, record a conversation about something unanticipated, or attach additional photos or mementos.

Let Pictures Tell a Story

If your dad has old photo albums or boxes full of memorabilia tucked away in a drawer, now is the time to bring them out! There are many places throughout the book for you and your dad to paste in photos and mementos and write captions.

Photos and mementos can spark a specific memory or evoke an important time or place. They also make it easy for you to ask him to share more details about a special moment. For example, you might want to know who appears in a picture and when and why it was taken. A ticket stub for a concert might prompt you to ask how your dad felt hearing his favorite songs played onstage. It's best to avoid getting bogged down in reviewing every single thing in your father's collection—that's a task that is better for another time.

Instead, let your father's response to each item guide you to the truly important ones.

Capturing the Conversations

While this book is designed to be a keepsake, don't worry too much about your messy handwriting or the cross-outs that will inevitably appear as you record your dad's answers. Remember that this book is not so much about the product that you will make. It is about the process of truly getting to know your dad and offering an opportunity for him to share his experiences. Feel free to converse and create your keepsake in a way that reflects that process—make notes and record immediate impressions directly on the page, write in between the lines, or doodle in the margins.

If you'd like this book to become a formal family keepsake, it might be helpful to jot down notes—particular phrases and words he uses, dates, and other specifics—on a separate piece of paper and then neatly transfer the gist of his answers into the book later. You can also consider using a recorder or camera to document your conversations. Just be sure to use a recording method that allows your dad to be completely comfortable and himself while answering the questions.

Picking and Choosing Questions

While there might be many questions that will resonate, not all of them will be relevant to your dad's life, or they might bring up topics that your dad might not want to discuss. You are always welcome to skip the ones that don't apply, modify the prompts to your liking, or use the space to answer another question.

You might also find that a question suggests a more specific, particular line of inquiry and lead you to create questions of your own. Perhaps your dad discovers a train of thought he wants to follow. Instead of working through the pages, you both might be inspired by the printed questions to devote a day to look through old photographs and record the memories in the "More Stories" pages at the back of the book (see page 106). Remember, these questions are a starting point for your conversation, not a script that you have to follow. Such serendipitous tangents often lead to the deepest memories or the most interesting revelations.

Your Arrival

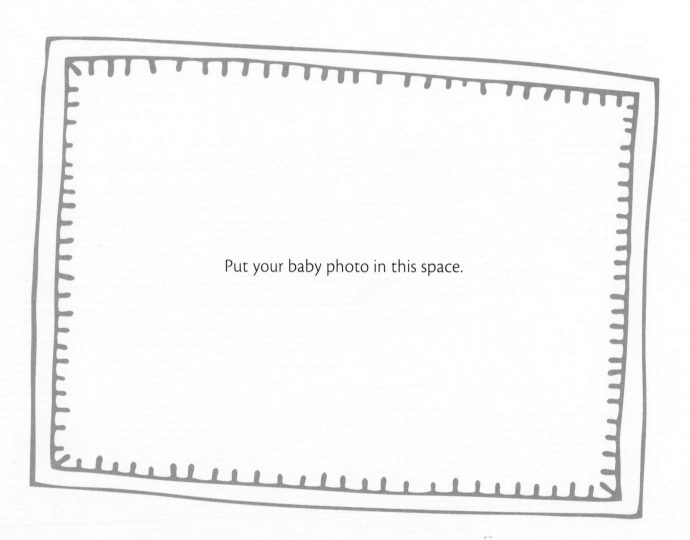

Put your baby photo in this space.

Full name: _____

Date of birth: _____

Place of birth: _____

Were you born at home or in a hospital? Who delivered you?

_____

_____

_____

_____

Was there anything unusual about your birth?

_____

_____

_____

_____

Who named you? Do your names have any special meaning?
Were you named after anyone?

_____

_____

_____

_____

Did you have any nicknames? How did you get them?

_____

_____

_____

_____

_____

Did your parents sing you a particular lullaby?
Did you have a special blanket or stuffed animal?

_____

_____

_____

_____

_____

How would your parents describe your personality as a baby?
Were you easygoing? Did you cry easily?

_____

_____

_____

_____

_____

Are there any stories about when you were a baby?

_____

_____

_____

_____

_____

_____

What is your very first memory?

_____

_____

_____

_____

_____

_____

What was your first word?

_____

_____

Your Roots

YOUR GRANDPARENTS

_____

_____

_____

_____

YOUR AUNTS AND UNCLES

_____

_____

_____

_____

_____

YOUR PARENTS

_____

_____

YOU

_____

YOUR SIBLINGS

_____

_____

_____

Where are our ancestors from?
When did they come to this country, and why?

_____

_____

_____

_____

_____

Where did they settle, and what did they do there?

_____

_____

_____

_____

_____

What stories do you know about them?

_____

_____

_____

_____

_____

Do you have any objects that belonged to an ancestor?

_____

_____

_____

_____

Do you know any relatives who speak a language other than English?

_____

_____

_____

_____

Have either of your parents identified strongly with his or her ethnic heritage or religion? How about you?

_____

_____

_____

_____

Who was the oldest relative you knew? What do you remember most about this person?

_____

_____

_____

_____

Who is the most famous (or infamous) person in your family?
Who is considered the most admired or the most interesting relative?
Are there any "black sheep"?

_____

_____

_____

_____

_____

Who is the best storyteller in your family?
What does this person talk about?

_____

_____

_____

_____

_____

Is there a trait associated with either your mom's or your dad's side of the family?
Do you think you possess it? Do I?

_____

_____

_____

_____

_____

Use these pages for pictures of your relatives from long ago.
What do you know about each person?

Name: _____

Birth date: _____

Place of birth: _____

Relationship to you: _____

About this person: _____

_____

_____

Name: _____

Birth date: _____

Place of birth: _____

Relationship to you: _____

About this person: _____

_____

_____

Name: _____

Birth date: _____

Place of birth: _____

Relationship to you: _____

About this person: _____

_____

_____

Are there any family traditions you practice that have been handed down for generations? Where did they come from?

_____

_____

_____

_____

_____

Which traditions do you want to pass down to me? Are there any new traditions that you've created?

_____

_____

_____

_____

_____

Your Family

••• Your Grandparents •••

Did you know your grandparents very well?
What do you remember most about them?

_____

_____

_____

_____

What did you call your grandparents? Where did these nicknames come from?

_____

_____

_____

_____

Where did they live? What were their homes like?

_____

_____

_____

_____

What were their lives like when they were young?
Where did they grow up?

_____

_____

_____

_____

_____

How did they make their living?

_____

_____

_____

_____

_____

What sort of parents were they?
How many children did they have?

_____

_____

_____

_____

_____

Use these pages for pictures of your grandparents.

Name: _____

Birth date: _____

Place of birth: _____

Name: _____

Birth date: _____

Place of birth: _____

Name: _____

Birth date: _____

Place of birth: _____

Name: _____

Birth date: _____

Place of birth: _____

How did you spend time with your grandparents?
Did they take you on little adventures? Did they cook anything special for you?

_____

_____

_____

_____

_____

_____

_____

_____

Did you have a favorite grandparent? Why?

_____

_____

_____

_____

_____

_____

_____

_____

What were the most important things that you learned from your grandparents?

_____

_____

_____

_____

_____

Did anyone ever tell you that you were like one of your grandparents?
How were you alike?

_____

_____

_____

_____

_____

What stories did your grandparents tell you?
Do you know any stories about them as well?

_____

_____

_____

_____

_____

••• Your Parents •••

Use these pages for pictures of your parents.

Name: _____

Birth date: _____

Place of birth: _____

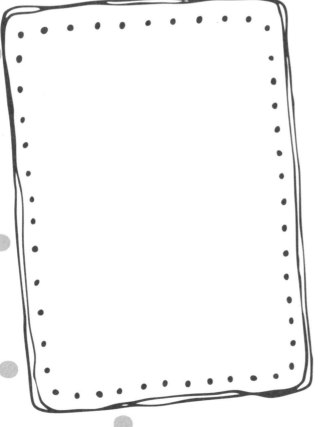

Name: _____

Birth date: _____

Place of birth: _____

Where did your parents grow up?
What were their childhoods like?

_____

_____

_____

_____

_____

_____

_____

_____

Do you know any stories about your parents when they were children?

_____

_____

_____

_____

_____

_____

_____

_____

How did your parents meet?
What do you think they liked best about each other?

_____

_____

_____

_____

If your parents were married, when did it happen?
Do you know any stories about their wedding?

_____

_____

_____

_____

_____

How did your parents enjoy spending their time together?

_____

_____

_____

_____

_____

What did your parents do to earn a living?
Did they like their jobs? Did you ever visit your parents at work?

_____

_____

_____

_____

_____

What were your parents' favorite hobbies?
Did they have any special talents, like playing the piano?

_____

_____

_____

_____

_____

How did you spend time with your parents?
Did you go on any outings with just your mom or dad?

_____

_____

_____

_____

_____

How are you like your parents? How are you different from them?

_____

_____

_____

_____

_____

How has your relationship with your parents changed? When you think about your parents now, do you see them differently than when you were a child?

_____

_____

_____

_____

_____

What is something you remember your parents teaching you?

_____

_____

_____

_____

_____

What's the best piece of advice that each parent has given you?

_____

_____

_____

_____

_____

What do you admire most about each parent?

_____

_____

_____

_____

_____

What character traits do you think your parents most wanted
their children to have?

_____

_____

_____

_____

_____

••● Your Siblings ●••

Use these pages for pictures of each of your siblings. If you were an only child, attach photos of people who acted like brothers and sisters, like cousins or best friends.

Name: _____

Birth date: _____

Place of birth: _____

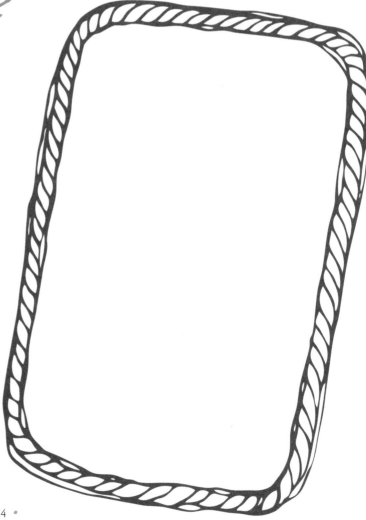

Name: _____

Birth date: _____

Place of birth: _____

Name: _____

Birth date: _____

Place of birth: _____

Name: _____

Birth date: _____

Place of birth: _____

What was the best thing about growing up in a family the size of yours?
What was the worst? Did you ever wish your family had been larger or smaller?

_____

_____

_____

_____

_____

Did you share a room with any of your siblings?
Did you get or give hand-me-down clothes? How did you feel about that?

_____

_____

_____

_____

_____

Did you and your siblings get along? What did you fight about?

_____

_____

_____

_____

_____

What was the biggest trouble that you and your siblings ever got in together?
What happened when your parents found out?

_____

_____

_____

_____

_____

What did you do for fun together?
What sort of adventures did you have?

_____

_____

_____

_____

_____

Who was the wildest child in the family? Who was the most generous?

_____

_____

_____

_____

_____

Tell me about a time that your brother or sister stood up for you.

_____

_____

_____

_____

_____

_____

_____

_____

Was there also a time when you risked something for a sibling?

_____

_____

_____

_____

_____

_____

_____

_____

_____

Did you have a favorite brother or sister?
Did you have a cousin or friend who seemed almost like a sibling?
What did you like best about that person?

_____

_____

_____

_____

_____

As you got older, who among your siblings do you think changed the most?

_____

_____

_____

_____

_____

Did you get closer to a sibling you'd not been that close with before?

_____

_____

_____

_____

_____

Growing Up

Where did you grow up? Did you live in a house or an apartment, or on a farm?

_____

_____

_____

_____

What was your bedroom like?
What did you see when you looked out your bedroom window?

_____

_____

_____

_____

Where did you spend most of your free time?
Did you have a place to hide out when you wanted to be alone?

_____

_____

_____

_____

When growing up, what were your favorite toys, games, books, or TV shows?
Did you take any lessons or play any sports?

_____

_____

_____

Who was your best friend? Who were some other good childhood friends?
If you could spend an afternoon with one of them today, who would it be, and why?

_____

_____

_____

What did you do for fun with your friends?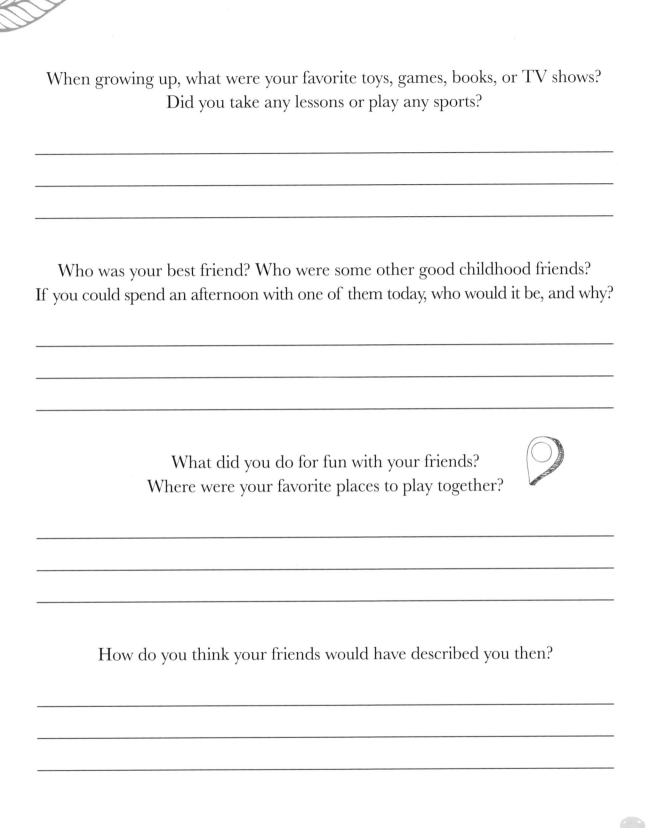
Where were your favorite places to play together?

_____

_____

_____

How do you think your friends would have described you then?

_____

_____

_____

What was your family life like? What were some household rules?
Were your parents strict?

_____

_____

_____

_____

_____

What were your chores? Did you have an allowance or a curfew?

_____

_____

_____

_____

_____

What did your family do for fun outings or vacations together?

_____

_____

_____

_____

_____

What was your favorite food as a kid? What food did you hate? Did your parents ever make you sit at the table until you had eaten everything on your plate?

_____

_____

_____

_____

_____

Did you have a favorite pet? How did you choose its name?

_____

_____

_____

_____

_____

Did you daydream about the future?
What did you think you were going to be when you grew up?

_____

_____

_____

_____

_____

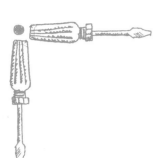

Who were your childhood heroes?
What did you admire most about them?

_____

_____

_____

_____

_____

What was the first really big responsibility you remember having, and
how did it make you feel?

_____

_____

_____

_____

_____

What was your biggest thrill as a kid?
What was the most trouble you ever got into?

_____

_____

_____

_____

_____

Use this page for photos and mementos of your childhood.

Education

SCHOOL: DATES OF ATTENDANCE:

_____

_____

_____

_____

_____

LIST YOUR AWARDS, HONORS, AND FAVORITE ACCOMPLISHMENTS:

_____

_____

_____

_____

_____

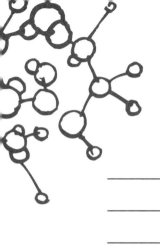

How old were you when you first started school?
Do you remember how you felt on your first day?

_____

_____

_____

_____

_____

What was your elementary school like?
What was your favorite part of the school day?
What did you do at lunchtime?

_____

_____

_____

_____

_____

How did you get to school? Did you walk to school or take a bus?
Did your parents pick you up and drop you off?

_____

_____

_____

_____

_____

Who was your first teacher? What do you remember about the class?

_____

_____

_____

_____

_____

When you were younger, what subjects were you good at?
Which ones did you hate? What was the hardest subject you had to master?

_____

_____

_____

_____

_____

Was there something you were better at than anyone in your class?
Did you win any awards? Did you participate in any science fairs or spelling bees?

_____

_____

_____

_____

_____

Use this page for photos and mementos of elementary school.

What was middle school like? How was it different from elementary school?
Did you take any interesting electives?

_____

_____

_____

_____

_____

Did you ever get sent to the principal or get in trouble?
What did your parents think?

_____

_____

_____

_____

_____

Did it scare you when you had to speak in front of the class?
Were you shy or outgoing?

_____

_____

_____

_____

_____

Use this page for photos and mementos of middle school.

What were you like in high school? Were you a good student?
Did you have many friends?

_____

_____

_____

_____

_____

_____

_____

_____

Did you play sports? Were you in any clubs or organizations?

_____

_____

_____

_____

_____

_____

_____

_____

Did you have to wear a uniform to school?
What were the popular clothes and hairstyles?

_____

_____

_____

_____

_____

What did you do as soon as you got out of school every day?
Did you work while you were going to school?
How much homework did you have?

_____

_____

_____

_____

_____

How did you spend your summer vacations?
Did you go to summer camp?

_____

_____

_____

_____

What were the biggest social events at your school?
Did you go to the prom or any formals?

_____

_____

_____

_____

_____

_____

_____

_____

What were some of the most fun (or wildest) things you and your friends did?

_____

_____

_____

_____

_____

_____

_____

_____

Use this page for photos and mementos of high school.

How do you think your classmates would have described you?
Did you win any superlatives in your yearbook?

_____

_____

_____

_____

Who was the most inspirational teacher you ever had?
What made this teacher special?

_____

_____

_____

_____

Which teachers did you fear or dislike the most?

_____

_____

_____

_____

What were the most important things that you learned inside
and outside the classroom?

_____

_____

_____

_____

_____

_____

_____

_____

What are some things that you wished you had learned in school?

_____

_____

_____

_____

_____

_____

_____

Testing Your Wings

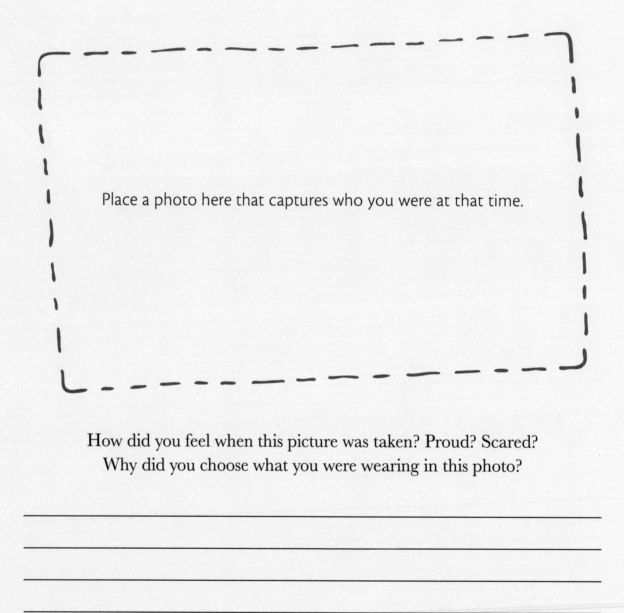

Place a photo here that captures who you were at that time.

How did you feel when this picture was taken? Proud? Scared?
Why did you choose what you were wearing in this photo?

_____

_____

_____

_____

_____

Was there a moment when you felt as if you were truly grown up:
Graduation? Your first job? Moving away from your family?

_____

_____

_____

_____

_____

_____

_____

_____

What was your dream for your future at this moment in your life?

_____

_____

_____

_____

_____

_____

_____

_____

What did you do right after high school?
Why did you make that choice?

_____

_____

_____

_____

_____

Did you attend college? Where did you go, and what did you study?
What was the most valuable thing that you learned?

_____

_____

_____

_____

_____

If you did not attend college, was that something you wanted to do?
Are you satisfied with how that choice turned out?

_____

_____

_____

_____

Use this page for photos and mementos of you as a young adult.

Describe your first . . .
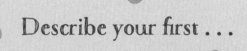

PAYCHECK: _____

_____

_____

BIG PURCHASE: _____

_____

_____

PLACE YOU LIVED ON YOUR OWN: _____

_____

_____

TRIP TAKEN BY YOURSELF: _____

_____

_____

PRESIDENTIAL CANDIDATE THAT YOU VOTED FOR: _____

_____

_____

Did you move out of your parents' house?
If you stayed at home, how did life with your parents change?

_____

_____

_____

_____

_____

What was your first place like? How did you decorate your space?
Did you live by yourself or with other people?

_____

_____

_____

_____

_____

When did you learn to drive? Who taught you, and how did that go?

_____

_____

_____

_____

What were some of your favorite things when you were a young adult?

BOOK (or other thing to read): _____

_____

MUSIC: _____

_____

PAYCHECK: _____

_____

MOVIE: _____

_____

TV SHOW: _____

_____

CELEBRITY: _____

_____

HOBBY: _____

_____

POLITICAL, SOCIAL, OR RELIGIOUS CAUSE: _____

_____

When did you cast your first vote? Was it exciting?
Who did you vote for, and why?

_____

_____

_____

_____

_____

Who was the first president that you remember?
What do you recall about this person's term?

_____

_____

_____

_____

_____

What were your parents' political and religious beliefs?
As you grew up, how did your beliefs differ from theirs?

_____

_____

_____

_____

_____

Was our country at war when you were young?
How do you think the war changed your life? Were you frightened?

_____

_____

_____

_____

_____

_____

_____

_____

Did you or anyone close to you enlist or work for any war efforts?
Tell me about those experiences, where you were,
what you did, and what you learned.

_____

_____

_____

_____

_____

_____

_____

_____

What are some of the jobs you've had?

COMPANY: DATES OF EMPLOYMENT:

_____

_____

_____

_____

_____

_____

_____

_____

_____

_____

What did you like about your earliest jobs? What did you dislike?
Were you good at what you did?

_____

_____

_____

_____

_____

How did you end up in your line of work?
Was there anything that happened when you were growing up that
influenced how you chose a particular field?

_____

_____

_____

_____

_____

If you could do it differently, would you choose a different line of work?

_____

_____

_____

_____

_____

How did you have fun? What did you do after work and on the weekends?
How about on your days off?

_____

_____

_____

_____

_____

What was most rewarding about the work you did?
What was the most challenging?

_____

_____

_____

_____

_____

Did you have to make any major career decisions?
Did you switch fields or turn down an opportunity to pursue something else?

_____

_____

_____

_____

_____

Have you retired yet? If so, what is your favorite part of retirement?
If you're still working, what part of retirement are you most looking forward to?

_____

_____

_____

_____

_____

Love and Relationships

Who was your first crush? Did this person like you back?

_____

_____

_____

_____

When did you have your first kiss?

_____

_____

_____

_____

Do you believe in love at first sight?

_____

_____

_____

_____

Describe your first date. Who was the person, and where did you go?
Did you ask the person out, or were you asked out?

_____

_____

_____

_____

_____

_____

_____

_____

Tell me about the best date you ever had. Was there a worst?
Where did you enjoy going on dates?

_____

_____

_____

_____

_____

_____

_____

_____

What was your first serious relationship like?
Can you tell me about your first breakup?

_____

_____

_____

_____

_____

_____

_____

_____

What lessons did you learn from your relationships?

_____

_____

_____

_____

_____

_____

_____

_____

_____

How did you meet my other parent? What was your first impression?

_____

_____

_____

_____

Where did you go on your first date? Was it fun?
Did you think you'd see each other again?

_____

_____

_____

_____

What did you like best about each other? Did you ever have a big argument?
How did you patch things up?

_____

_____

_____

_____

••◐ Your Wedding ◑••

When you decided to get married, who proposed, and how did it happen?
What did your family and friends say when they heard the news?
How long were you engaged?

_____

_____

_____

_____

_____

Date: _____

Place: _____

Number of guests: _____

Members of the wedding party: _____

_____

_____

_____

_____

Song for first dance: _____

Use this page for photos and mementos of your wedding.

What was the best moment of your wedding day?
Was there a worst or scariest?

_____

_____

_____

_____

_____

Where did you go on your honeymoon?

_____

_____

_____

_____

_____

Describe the first place you lived together as a married couple.
Was it fun to set up your household? How did you split up chores?

_____

_____

_____

_____

_____

What are your favorite parts about being married?

_____

_____

_____

_____

_____

What are the most challenging?

_____

_____

_____

_____

_____

How has your relationship with your spouse changed?
Is there anything you learned about your spouse that surprised you?

_____

_____

_____

_____

_____

Becoming a Parent

Place your children's' baby pictures here.

Name: _____

Birth date: _____

Place of birth: _____

Name: _____

Birth date: _____

Place of birth: _____

Name: _____

Birth date: _____

Place of birth: _____

Name: _____

Birth date: _____

Place of birth: _____

When you imagined having a family, how many children did you want?
How do you feel about the size of our family now?

_____

_____

_____

_____

_____

_____

_____

_____

How did you react when you discovered your first child was on the way?
Who were the first people that you told?

_____

_____

_____

_____

_____

_____

_____

_____

In the movies, there's often a dramatic rush to the hospital
for the birth of a baby. What was it really like for you?
What do you remember most about the births of each of us?

_____

_____

_____

_____

_____

What did you think when you saw each of us for the first time?

_____

_____

_____

_____

_____

Tell me about how you named us. Did we have any nicknames?

_____

_____

_____

_____

_____

What were the most difficult and the most frightening things about
suddenly being responsible for little ones?
What were the most surprising and delightful ones?

_____

_____

_____

_____

_____

What are some things you liked best about parenting us when we were younger?

_____

_____

_____

_____

_____

What do you think was your best trait as a parent?

_____

_____

_____

_____

_____

Use this page for photos and mementos of our family when we were small children.

For each of your children, tell me what you think is his or her greatest strength. Are any of us more like you? Do you think aliens may have brought one of us?

_____

_____

_____

_____

_____

What did you think each one of us was sure to be when we grew up?
Who surprised you the most with how they turned out?

_____

_____

_____

_____

_____

If you could change something about the way we grew up, what would it be?

_____

_____

_____

_____

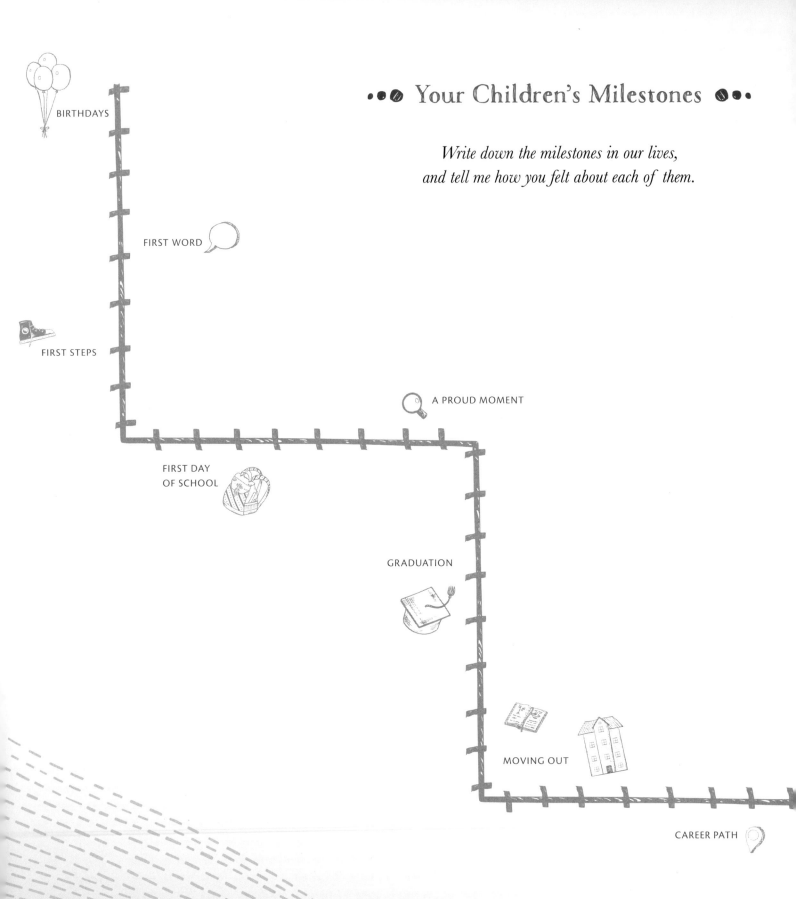

Your Children's Milestones

Write down the milestones in our lives,
and tell me how you felt about each of them.

BIRTHDAYS

FIRST WORD

FIRST STEPS

FIRST STEPS

A PROUD MOMENT

FIRST DAY
OF SCHOOL

GRADUATION

MOVING OUT

CAREER PATH

How has parenting changed now that we have become older?
Did you start a career, go back to school, or do something
you didn't have the time for before?

_____

_____

_____

_____

_____

Are you now an empty nester?
What do you miss about us living at home?

_____

_____

_____

_____

_____

How do you think parenting in general has changed in your lifetime?
Are these changes good or bad?

_____

_____

_____

_____

_____

Family Fun

How would you describe our family?
Close-knit? Independent? Rambunctious? Funny?

_____

_____

_____

_____

_____

_____

_____

What is our family's best characteristic as a group?

_____

_____

_____

_____

_____

_____

What are some holidays that our family celebrates?

HOLIDAY: DATE:

_____

_____

_____

_____

_____

_____

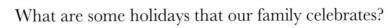

When you were young, what was your favorite holiday?
How did you decorate? Did you get to stay up late or eat special foods?

_____

_____

_____

_____

_____

_____

How did you celebrate your birthday when you were little?
How did that influence our family traditions?

_____

_____

_____

_____

_____

What were your favorite holidays when we were little kids?
What about now?

_____

_____

_____

_____

Tell me about some family celebrations you vividly remember.

_____

_____

_____

_____

Are there any special family recipes that you want to share with me?

RECIPE NAME: _____

INGREDIENTS: INSTRUCTIONS:

_____   _____

_____   _____

_____   _____

_____   _____

_____   _____

_____   _____

_____   _____

RECIPE NAME: _____

INGREDIENTS: INSTRUCTIONS:

_____   _____

_____   _____

_____   _____

_____   _____

_____   _____

_____   _____

_____   _____

What is the best family vacation that you can remember?
What was the most disastrous?

_____

_____

_____

_____

_____

What kinds of family outings did we enjoy?
Did we have any activities that we liked do together on a regular basis?

_____

_____

_____

_____

_____

What games did we like to play as a family?
What were some of the ways we had fun together that you particularly enjoyed?

_____

_____

_____

_____

_____

Use this page for photos and mementos of family celebrations and outings.

Here and Now

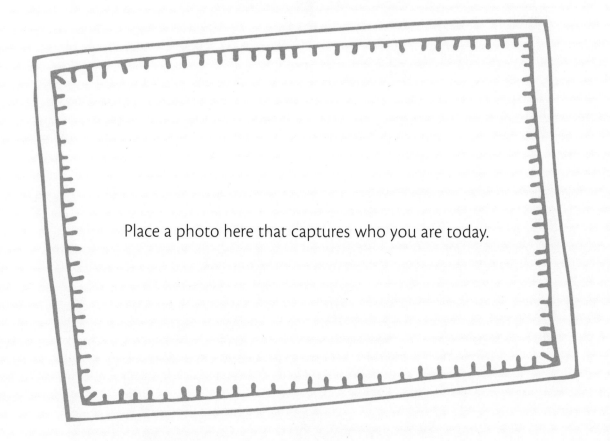

Place a photo here that captures who you are today.

How did you feel when this picture was taken?
How is it different from how you felt in the photo on page 58?
Why did you choose what you were wearing in this photo?

_____

_____

_____

_____

_____

Where do you live today? What is it like?
How has your current town or city changed since you first moved here?

_____

_____

_____

_____

_____

What is your daily routine like? What are the favorite parts of your day?
How does your typical day today compare to your typical day in the past?

_____

_____

_____

_____

_____

What's your favorite way to spend free time?
Do you participate in any organizations or activities?
Who are the people you socialize with the most?

_____

_____

_____

_____

_____

What are some of your favorite things now?

BOOK (or other thing to read): _____

_____

MUSIC: _____

_____

MOVIE: _____

_____

TV SHOW: _____

_____

CELEBRITY: _____

_____

HOBBY: _____

_____

POLITICAL, SOCIAL, OR RELIGIOUS CAUSE: _____

_____

How have your interests changed over time?
What sorts of things have become more important to you? Less?

_____

_____

_____

_____

_____

_____

_____

_____

How would you describe your political and religious beliefs?
Have they changed since you were a young adult?
Do you think they will continue to evolve?

_____

_____

_____

_____

_____

_____

_____

_____

Reflections

What accomplishment in your life do you feel is the most significant?
What are some other things that you're proud of?

_____

_____

_____

_____

What do you admire most about yourself? What are your best qualities?

_____

_____

_____

_____

Who are the people who have most influenced you? Why?

_____

_____

_____

_____

Describe your biggest adventure. Have you traveled anywhere memorable? Have you had any experiences that other people might not have?

_____

_____

_____

_____

_____

_____

_____

What's the biggest risk that you've taken?

_____

_____

_____

_____

_____

_____

_____

What were the most important historical events in your lifetime?
When these moments happened, where were you? What were you doing?

_____

_____

_____

_____

_____

What do you think are the three most important inventions of your lifetime?
What new technology had the most impact on your life personally?

_____

_____

_____

_____

_____

In what ways have social norms changed in your lifetime?
What do you think about these changes?
Is there anything that you think has changed for the better or worse?

_____

_____

_____

_____

_____

Of the famous people of your lifetime—politicians, artists, athletes, celebrities, spiritual leaders—who are the three that you think had the greatest impact on the world at large? How do you think they changed things?

_____

_____

_____

_____

_____

_____

_____

_____

If you could have a conversation with one important person, living or dead, who would you choose? What would you want to know?

_____

_____

_____

_____

_____

_____

_____

_____

If you had the opportunities that your children have, what would you have chosen to do differently in your life? How do you think that might have changed who you are today?

_____

_____

_____

_____

_____

_____

_____

What advantages do you think you had that your children don't?

_____

_____

_____

_____

_____

_____

_____

Look again at what you said was your dream for the future on page 59.
How close do you think you've come to it? Are you disappointed or glad about
the ways your life may have turned out differently from that dream?

_____

_____

_____

_____

_____

_____

_____

What do you look forward to most in the future?
What do you think the world will look like?

_____

_____

_____

_____

_____

_____

_____

Collected Wisdom

What is the key to having a good life?

_____

_____

_____

_____

_____

What are some important principles and values to live by?

_____

_____

_____

_____

_____

What do you recommend doing if you're facing a tough decision or
if you're uncertain about the future?

_____

_____

_____

_____

_____

What are the best ways to handle failure? What about success?

_____

_____

_____

_____

What should you do when you've lost something or someone important to you?

_____

_____

_____

_____

What is something that many people make a big deal about but
isn't that important after all?

_____

_____

_____

_____

What are some things you keep in mind when you're taking a risk or doing something that you've never done before?

_____

_____

_____

_____

_____

What makes for a good job? Is it the salary, enjoying the work, making a contribution to the community, or something else?

_____

_____

_____

_____

_____

What traits should you seek in a friend?

_____

_____

_____

_____

_____

What do you think are the keys to a good relationship or marriage?
What traits would you advise your children to seek in a partner?

_____

_____

_____

_____

What is your best parenting advice?

_____

_____

_____

_____

What would you like to say to your children, grandchildren,
and future generations?

_____

_____

_____

_____

More Stories

Use these pages to share more stories or record anything else that you want to tell me.

CONTINUED FROM PAGE _____

_____

_____

_____

_____

CONTINUED FROM PAGE _____

_____

_____

_____

_____

CONTINUED FROM PAGE _____

_____

_____

_____

_____

CONTINUED FROM PAGE _____

CONTINUED FROM PAGE _____

CONTINUED FROM PAGE _____

Add more photos and mementos on the next few pages.